Your Favorite Authors

Shel Silverstein

by Molly Kolpin

CAPSTONE PRESS
a capstone imprint

First Facts are published by Capstone Press,
1710 Roe Crest Drive, North Mankato, Minnesota 56003
www.capstonepub.com

Library of Congress Cataloging-in-Publication Data
Kolpin, Molly.
  Shel Silverstein / by Molly Kolpin.
      pages cm.—(First Facts. Your Favorite Authors)
  Includes bibliographical references and index.
  Summary: "Presents the life and career of Shel Silverstein, including his childhood, education, and milestones as a best-selling children's author"—Provided by publisher.
  ISBN 978-1-4765-0224-3 (library binding)
  ISBN 978-1-4765-3439-8 (paperback)
  ISBN 978-1-4765-3421-3 (eBook PDF)
1. Silverstein, Shel—Juvenile literature. 2. Authors, American—20th century—Biography—Juvenile literature. 3. Children's stories—Authorship—Juvenile literature. I. Title.
  PS3569.I47224Z73 2014
  818'.5409—dc23
  [B]   2013003121

Editorial Credits
Christopher L. Harbo, editor; Tracy Davies McCabe and Gene Bentdahl, designers;
Marcie Spence, media researcher; Kathy McColley, production specialist

Photo Credits
Alamy Images: Everett Collection Historical, 15; Capstone: Michael Byers, cover, 11 (bottom); Capstone Studio: Karon Dubke, 13 (top), 17, 19; Corbis: Jeff Albertson, 13 (bottom); Getty Images: Gems/Redferns, 21; Photo by Larry Moyer. © Evil Eye, LLC. All rights reserved. Used by permission., 5, 9; Shutterstock: Alena Hovorkova, design element, anfisa focusova, design element, Canicula, design element, Gorbash Varvara, design element, KonstantinChristian, 11 (top left), SergiyN, 7, Tena Rebernjak, design element, vectorgirl, 11 (top right)

Printed in the United States of America in North Mankato, Minnesota.
042013   007223CGF13

Table of Contents

Chapter 1: Breaking Ground

Shel Silverstein surprised the children's **publishing** world in 1964. His book, *The Giving Tree*, was finally being published. This story about a boy and a tree had been **rejected** by many publishers. They thought it was too sad for a children's book. But *The Giving Tree* sold millions of copies. Silverstein's career as a children's author took off.

---

publishing—having to do with producing and distributing a book, magazine, or newspaper so that people can buy it

reject—to refuse to accept something, such as an idea, drawing, or book

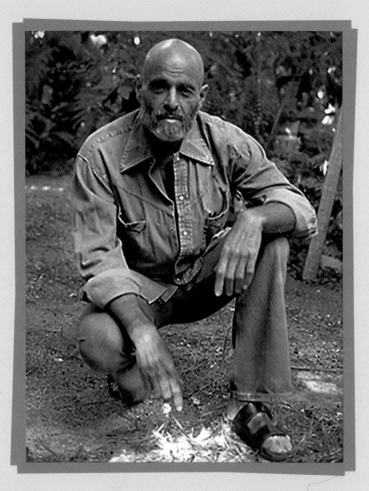

"If you're behind the times, they won't notice you. If you're right in tune with them ... they won't care much for you. Be just a little ahead of them."
—Shel Silverstein on being an original writer

Chapter 2: Perfecting His Craft

Sheldon Allan Silverstein's birth date is a mystery. Some sources say he was born September 25, 1930. Others say the year was 1932. Either way, he was born in Chicago, Illinois. As a child, Shel dreamed of playing baseball for the Chicago White Sox. But he was not a good athlete. Instead he turned to drawing. He studied art at two colleges in Chicago.

Chicago, Illinois

Silverstein was **drafted** into the
U.S. Army in 1953. While overseas
he worked for a military newspaper.
Silverstein often drew cartoons for
the newspaper that poked fun at his
superiors. Sometimes the cartoons got
Silverstein into trouble. But no matter
what others thought, Silverstein insisted
on staying true to himself.

---

draft—to select young men to serve in
the military

superior—someone who has a higher rank
or position than others

Shel on Creativity

Even when Silverstein was a famous author, not everyone liked his work. But Silverstein ignored his critics. "I think that if you're a creative person, you should … do your work and not care about how it's received," Silverstein said.

After Silverstein left the Army, he became a **cartoonist** for newspapers and magazines. He also began writing and recording music.

Silverstein's life changed forever in 1963. His friend Tomi Ungerer talked Silverstein into meeting with **editor** Ursula Nordstrom. Ungerer and Nordstrom suggested that Silverstein try writing for children.

---

cartoonist—a person who draws cartoons

editor—someone who checks the content of a book and gets it ready to be published

"I never planned to write or draw for kids. It was Tomi Ungerer ... who insisted—practically dragged me, kicking and screaming into Ursula Nordstrom's office."—Shel Silverstein

Chapter 3: Constantly Creating

Silverstein finished his first children's book in 1963. *Lafcadio, The Lion Who Shot Back* was about a lion that leaves the jungle. Lafcadio has adventures in the city as an expert shot with a gun.

While writing the story, Silverstein was not sure children's books were right for him. But Nordstrom believed in him. She worked with Silverstein to make his writing easier for children to read.

It turned out that children's books were perfect for Silverstein's writing and drawing talents. He published four more children's books in 1964. Three were picture books. *Who Wants a Cheap Rhinoceros? By Uncle Shelby* came first. *The Giving Tree* and *Uncle Shelby's A Giraffe and a Half* soon followed. *Uncle Shelby's Zoo: Don't Bump the Glump!* was Silverstein's first collection of **poems**.

---

poem—a piece of writing set out in short lines, often with a rhythm or rhyme

Uncle Shelby

Silverstein's name is now famous. But many of his children's books were published under the name Uncle Shelby. Silverstein did not want to appear as a strict parent or teacher. Instead, he wanted readers to see him as a fun-loving uncle.

Silverstein wrote another poetry collection called *Where the Sidewalk Ends* in 1974. The book's **illustrations** and funny **rhymes** were an instant hit with young readers.

Silverstein gained even more fans in 1981 with *A Light in the Attic.* This book also had silly poems. It became the first children's book to make *The New York Times* best-seller list.

---

illustration—a drawing in a book or magazine

rhyme—word endings that sound the same

"I would hope that people, no matter what age, would find something to identify with in my books."—Shel Silverstein

Silverstein is best known for his children's books. But he worked mostly as a cartoonist, songwriter, and **playwright** later in life. He returned to children's publishing in 1996. He released a book of poems titled *Falling Up*. He also created an activity book called *Draw a Skinny Elephant* in 1998. Silverstein died unexpectedly May 10, 1999.

---

playwright—a person who writes plays

Chapter 4: Making His Mark

During his lifetime Silverstein released 11 children's books. Two more of his children's books were published after his death. *Runny Babbit* was released in 2005. *Every Thing On It* hit bookstores in 2011. Though Silverstein is no longer with us, his incredible stories live on. They continue to earn him new fans.

"I want to go everywhere, look at and listen to everything. You can go crazy with some of the wonderful stuff there is in life."—Shel Silverstein

Timeline

1930?	born September 25 in Chicago, Illinois; some sources say he was born in 1932
1953	drafted into the U.S. Army
1963	first children's book, *Lafcadio, The Lion Who Shot Back,* is published
1964	*Who Wants a Cheap Rhinoceros? By Uncle Shelby, The Giving Tree, Uncle Shelby's A Giraffe and a Half,* and *Uncle Shelby's Zoo: Don't Bump the Glump!* are published
1970	has a daughter, Shoshanna, with Susan Hastings
1974	*Where the Sidewalk Ends* is published
1976	*The Missing Piece* is published
1981	*A Light in the Attic* and *The Missing Piece Meets the Big O* are published
1982	daughter dies at age 11 from a brain aneurysm
1984	has a son, Matthew, with Sarah Spencer
1996	*Falling Up* is published
1998	*Draw a Skinny Elephant* is published
1999	dies May 10 in Key West, Florida
2005	*Runny Babbit* is published
2011	*Every Thing On It* is published

Glossary

cartoonist (kar-TOON-ist)—a person who draws cartoons

draft (DRAFT)—to select young men to serve in the military

editor (ED-uh-tur)—someone who checks the content of a book and gets it ready to be published

illustration (il-uh-STRAY-shuhn)—a drawing in a book or magazine

playwright (PLAY-rite)—a person who writes plays

poem (POH-uhm)—a piece of writing set out in short lines, often with a rhythm or rhyme

publishing (PUHB-lish-ing)—having to do with producing and distributing a book, magazine, or newspaper so that people can buy it

reject (ri-JEKT)—to refuse to accept something, such as an idea, drawing, or book

rhyme (RIME)—word endings that sound the same

superior (suh-PIHR-ee-ur)—someone who has a higher rank or position than others

Read More

Baughan, **Michael Gray**. *Shel Silverstein*. Who Wrote That? New York: Chelsea House, 2008.

Lynette, **Rachel**. *Shel Silverstein*. Inventors and Creators. San Diego, Calif.: KidHaven Press, 2006.

Internet Sites

FactHound offers a safe, fun way to find Internet sites related to this book. All of the sites on FactHound have been researched by our staff.

Here's all you do:

Visit *www.facthound.com*

Type in this code: 9781476502243

Check out projects, games and lots more at
www.capstonekids.com

Super-cool stuff!